1 MONTH OF
FREE
READING

at
www.ForgottenBooks.com

By purchasing this book you are eligible for one month membership to ForgottenBooks.com, giving you unlimited access to our entire collection of over 1,000,000 titles via our web site and mobile apps.

To claim your free month visit:
www.forgottenbooks.com/free953560

ISBN 978-0-260-51989-4
PIBN 10953560

This book is a reproduction of an important historical work. Forgotten Books uses
state-of-the-art technology to digitally reconstruct the work, preserving the original format
whilst repairing imperfections present in the aged copy. In rare cases, an imperfection in
the original, such as a blemish or missing page, may be replicated in our edition. We do,
however, repair the vast majority of imperfections successfully; any imperfections that
remain are intentionally left to preserve the state of such historical works.

Historic, archived document

Do not assume content reflects current
scientific knowledge, policies, or practices.

2F

June 1957

FOR RELEASE
JUNE 28, A. M.

The
WHEAT
SITUATION

WS-154

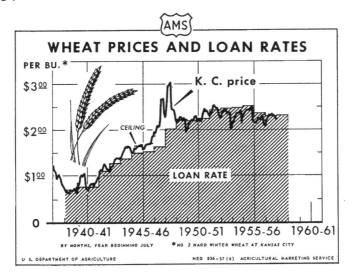

AMS

WHEAT PRICES AND LOAN RATES

PER BU. *

$3⁰⁰

K. C. price

$2⁰⁰

CEILING

$1⁰⁰

LOAN RATE

0

1940-41   1945-46   1950-51   1955-56   1960-61

BY MONTHS, YEAR BEGINNING JULY   * NO 2 HARD WINTER WHEAT AT KANSAS CITY

U S. DEPARTMENT OF AGRICULTURE   NEG 836-57 (6)   AGRICULTURAL MARKETING SERVICE

With the minimum national average support price for 1958-crop wheat announced at $1.78, the support would be down 22 cents from $2.00 for the 1957 crop. Supports have declined in only 3 years since the support programs were started in 1938.

In 1955-56, the year most like 1957-58, the low monthly average for No. 2 Hard Winter Wheat at Kansas City came in August and the high in April. In 1948, the low was also in August, but in 1954, when the season was not as late as in 1957, it was in June. The high monthly average in 1954-55 occurred in May, and while the high month in 1948-49 was in December, April was only slightly lower than December.

Published five times a year by

AGRICULTURAL MARKETING SERVICE

UNITED STATES DEPARTMENT OF AGRICULTURE

Table 1 .- Wheat: Loan rate, actual price to growers, supply and distribution factors, quantity pledged and delivered to CCC, stocks owned by CCC and loans outstanding, 1938-57

Year beginning July	Gross loan rate	Average actual price to growers 1/	Price above loan	Supply and distribution factors				Under price support
				Total domestic supply 2/	Domestic disappear-ance 3/	Net exports 4/	Year-end carryover	
	Dollars	Dollars	Dollars	Million bushels	Million bushels	Million bushels	Million bushels	Million bushels
1938	0.59	0.56	-0.03	1,073	713	110	250	85.7
1939	.63	.69	.06	991	662	49	280	167.7
1940	.64	.67	.03	1,094	675	34	385	278.4
1941	.98	.94	-.04	1,327	667	29	631	366.3
1942	1.14	1.09	-.05	1,600	949	32	619	408.1
1943	1.23	1.35	.12	1,463	1,237	5/-91	317	130.2
1944	1.35	1.41	.06	1,377	992	106	279	180.4
1945	1.38	1.49	.11	1,387	894	393	100	59.7
1946	1.49	1.90	.41	1,252	766	402	84	22.0
1947	1.84	2.29	.45	1,443	757	490	196	31.2
1948	2.00	1.98	-.02	1,491	678	506	307	6/366.0
1949	1.95	1.88	-.07	1,406	680	301	425	6/380.8
1950	1.99	2.00	.01	1,444	686	358	400	6/196.9
1951	2.18	2.11	7/-.07	1,388	684	448	256	6/212.9
1952	2.20	2.09	7/-.11	1,562	656	300	606	6/459.9
1953	2.21	2.04	7/-.17	1,779	630	215	934	6/557.2
1954	2.24	2.12	7/-.12	1,917	607	274	1,036	6/430.7
1955	2.08	1.99	7/-.09	1,971	598	340	1,033	6/320.7
1956 8/	2.00	1.97	7/-.03	2,030	596	531	903	6/252.2
1957 8/	2.00			(1,874)	(595)	(399)	(880)	

	Delivered to CCC 9/	CCC stocks and loans outstanding at year-end (June 30)				
		Stocks owned by CCC 10/	Under loan			Total
			Crop previous July 11/	Crops of earlier years		
	Million bushels	Million bushels	Million bushels	Million bushels		Million bushels
1938	15.7	6.6	21.5	---		28.1
1939	7.7	1.6	10.3	---		11.9
1940	173.7	169.2	31.4	7.2		207.8
1941	269.8	319.7	98.1	1.4		419.2
1942	184.0	259.8	133.3	4.9		398.0
1943	0.3	99.1	15.5	2.5		117.1
1944	72.9	103.7	20.1	1.9		125.7
1945	.2	---	32.5	---		32.5
1946	---	---	0.7	---		0.7
1947	---	---	.8	---		.8
1948	290.9	227.2	16.3	---		243.5
1949	247.5	327.7	28.5	5.0		361.2
1950	41.9	196.4	8.9	2.3		207.6
1951	91.3	143.3	11.6	---		154.9
1952	397.7	470.0	22.5	---		492.5
1953	486.1	774.6	71.4	3.9		849.9
1954	391.6	975.9	11.3	2.8		990.0
1955 8/	267.8	950.7	11/27.6	1.3		979.6
1956	12/124.4					

1/ United States marketing year prices are the result of (1) weighting State monthly prices by monthly sales to obtain State marketing-year averages, and (2) weighting the State marketing-year averages by total sales for each State. Includes an allowance for unredeemed loans at average loan values beginning 1938. 2/ Beginning carryover plus production. 3/ Total supply minus net exports minus year-end carryover. 4/ Includes shipments to United States Territories of about 4 million bushels annually. 5/ Exports totaled 45 million bushels and imports used to supplement domestic animal feed supplies totaled 136 million bushels. 6/ Includes the following quantities put under purchase agreements in million bushels, beginning in 1948, as follows: 1948-crop wheat, 112.0; 1949-crop wheat, 45.5; 1950-crop wheatn, 8.6; 1951-crop wheat, 13.4; 1952-crop wheat, 61.3; 1953-crop wheat, 63.2; 1954-crop wheat, 29.5; 1955-crop wheat, 43.5 and 1956-crop wheat 18.5. 7/ Growers assumed storage charges which averaged 7 to 10 cents per bushel, depending on the time it was put under loan. 8/ Preliminary. 9/ Includes purchase agreement wheat delivered to CCC. 10/ Includes open-market purchases, if any, beginning in 1943, and accordingly may include some new-crop wheat.   11/ For example, 27.6 million bushels are 1955-crop wheat under loan on June 30, 1956; 2.8 million bushels were under loan from earlier crops. Any 1956 crop is not included. 12/ Through May 31, 1957.

- - -   - - - - -   - - - - - - -
T H E   W H E A T   S I T U A T I O N
- - -   - - - - -   - - - - - - - -

Approved by the Outlook and Situation Board, June 24, 1957

CONTENTS

SUMMARY

The total wheat supply for the marketing year beginning July 1, 1957 is now estimated at about 1,880 million bushels, 8 percent less than the 2,038 million a year earlier. The decrease results from the first substantial reduction in the carryover since 1952 and a small decline in production this year.

Very large exports account for the reduction in the carryover. United States exports of wheat and flour during the marketing year ending June 30, 1957 are expected to total a record high of about 535 million bushels, compared with 346 million bushels a year earlier. The previous record high was 504 million bushels shipped in 1948. Large exports are due primarily to special export programs such as Public Law 480 and increased demand from Europe as a result of short crops in 1956.

The July 1, 1957 carryover is expected to be 900 million bushels, or slightly more, on the basis of April 1 stocks and estimated domestic disappearance and exports in May and June. This would be down about 130 million bushels from a year earlier. The official estimate of stocks of old-crop wheat in all positions on July 1 will be released on July 24. The bulk of the carryover again will be held by the Commodity Credit

Corporation. In addition to carryover, the supply for the 1957-58 marketing year includes this year's crop, forecast at 971 million bushels as of June 1, and imports of about 5 million bushels, mostly feeding quality wheat.

Domestic disappearance for 1957-58 is estimated at about 600 million bushels. If exports in 1957-58 exceed 380 million bushels, the carryover July 1, 1958 would be correspondingly reduced.

Favorable moisture conditions are resulting in prospects for record wheat yields this year. The prospective crop is only 3 percent smaller than last year's crop, despite the 12.8 million acres of wheat land placed in the Soil Bank Acreage Reserve.

Analysis of prospective supply and distribution by classes indicates continued vary large supplies of hard red winter wheat and abundant supplies of hard red spring wheat. Prospective supplies of durum are more than sufficient to meet domestic requirements, and those of soft red winter are ample for sizable exports and domestic needs.

Cash wheat prices have been declining seasonally, though delayed combining and some concern over damage because of wet fields in the Southwest have resulted in temporary price increases.

In the 1957-58 marketing year, the average price to growers may again average near the national support level. In 1955-56, the price to growers averaged $1.99, which is 9 cents under the national average loan rate of $2.08, but in 1956-57 with an estimated average price of $1.97, it is only 3 cents below the announced loan of $2.00. The higher price, compared with the loan, reflects the fact that much of the wheat exported this year was purchased in the commercial market. The extent to which Southwest wheat is of high moisture content will be a factor in determining how near prices will average to the $2.00 support level for 1957-58. High moisture content may result in much of the crop being sold after harvest rather than being held for price support.

Preliminary returns from the referendum held on June 20 in the 36-State wheat producing area show that 83.3 percent of farmers voting favored marketing quotas for the 1958 wheat crop. Approval by two-thirds or more makes quotas effective.

With this approval, producers in the 36-commercial wheat States, who stay within the acreages allotted for their farms, will be eligible for the full level of price support which is set at a minimum national average of $1.78 per bushel. In noncommercial States, the wheat price support will be at 75 percent of the rate computed on the basis of the $1.78 national average.

Preliminary data indicate that world wheat exports in 1956-57, estimated at 1,210 million bushels, will exceed the previous record of 1,066 million in 1951-52 by nearly 150 million bushels. Exports at this level will be 17 percent above 1955-56 and 29 percent above the 1946-55 average of 941 million bushels. The larger world wheat exports indicated for 1956-57 reflect much larger exports from the United States, a substantial increase from Australia, but decreases in exports from Canada and Argentina.

The outlook for the 1957 wheat crop in Northern Hemisphere countries is generally favorable, on the basis of preliminary indications. Better prospects are reported for most parts of Europe and also for the countries of Asia for which reports are available.

THE DOMESTIC WHEAT SITUATION

1957-58 Supply Prospects Down About 8 percent; July 1, 1958 Carryover May be Down Slightly

The total wheat supply for the marketing year beginning July 1, 1957 is now estimated at 1,879 million bushels, 8 percent less than the 2,038 million a year earlier. With the crop as currently estimated down only 26 million bushels, the reduction is largely the result of the smaller carryover, which reflects record large exports in 1956-57.

On the basis of April 1 stocks and estimated domestic disappearance and exports in May and June, the July 1, 1957 carryover is expected to be about 903 million bushels. The official estimate of stocks of old-crop wheat in all positions on July 1 will be released on July 24. The bulk of the carryover will again be held by CCC.

In addition to the carryover, the supply for the 1957-58 marketing year consists of a crop forecast at 971 million bushels as of June 1, and an allowance for imports of 1 million bushels of milling wheat (limited by quota) and 4 million bushels of feeding quality wheat. Total imports of about 8 million bushels are indicated for 1956-57.

Domestic disappearance for 1957-58 is estimated at about 600 million bushels. Civilian and military food use (including use by Territories of the United States) is expected to be about 482 million bushels, feed use of about 60 million and seed use of about 57 million.

A domestic disappearance of 600 million bushels would leave about 1,280 million bushels for export during the marketing year and carryover at the end of the year. Assuming exports of about 400 million bushels, the carryover July 1, 1958 on this basis would total about 880 million bushels, slightly less than on July 1, 1957. Table 2 shows wheat supply and distribution, 1951-57.

Record yields per acre resulted from favorable moisture conditions in major producing areas. Had it not been for the acreage placed in the Soil Bank the crop would have been much larger and carryover on July 1, 1958 substantially increased. As of May 17, farmers had signed up 12,783,192 acre of wheat under the Program. This acreage includes winter wheat agreements signed last fall, less cancellations, plus spring wheat agreements signed through May 17. 1/

Table 2.- Wheat: Supply and distribution, United States,
1951-56 and 1957 projected

Item	Year beginning July						
	1951	1952	1953	1954	1955	1956 1/	1957 2/
	Mil. bu.	Mil. bu.	Mil. bu.	Mil. bu.	Mil. bu.	Mil. bu.	Mil. bu.
Supply							
Carryover on July 1	399.9	256.0	605.5	933.5	1,036.2	1,033	903
Production	988.2	1,306.4	1,173.1	983.9	934.7	997	971
Imports 3/	31.6	21.6	5.5	4.2	9.9	8	5
Total	1,419.7	1,584.0	1,784.1	1,921.6	1,980.8	2,038	1,879
Domestic disappearance							
Food 4/	496.5	488.4	487.1	486.0	480.9	483	482
Seed	88.2	89.1	69.5	64.8	67.7	57	57
Industry	.9	.2	.2	.2	.7	---	---
Feed 5/	102.8	83.0	76.8	60.0	52.2	60	60
Total	688.4	660.7	633.6	611.0	601.5	600	599
Exports 6/	475.3	317.8	217.0	274.4	345.9	535	7/400
Total disappearance	1,163.7	978.5	850.6	885.4	947.4	1,135	7/999
Stocks on June 30	256.0	605.5	933.5	1,036.2	1,033.4	903	880

1/ Preliminary.
2/ Projected.
3/ Excludes imports of wheat for milling-in-bond and export as flour.
4/ Includes shipments to United States territories and military food use at home and abroad.
5/ This is the residual figure, after all other disappearance is accounted for.
6/ Actual exports including those for civilian feeding under the military supply program.
7/ Very tentative.

1/ Maximum payments on this acreage would total $230,851,526 on 233,004 signed agreements. This represents an average of $18.06 per acre and an average of $990.76 per agreement.

ALL WHEAT: PERCENT ACREAGE RESERVE SIGNED THRU APRIL 19, 1957 OF ALLOTTED ACRES

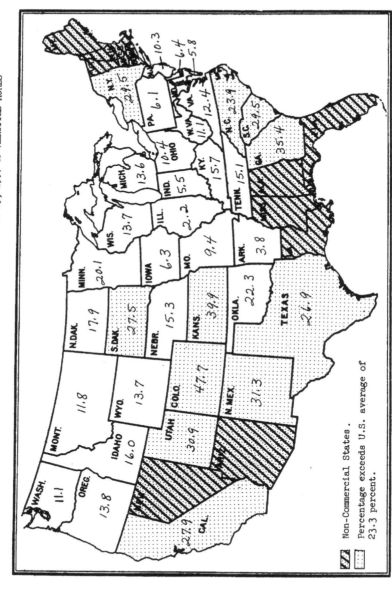

Non-Commercial States.

Percentage exceeds U.S. average of 23.3 percent.

CSS. Soil Bank Division

All Wheat Production 3 Percent
Below 1956; Winter About
Same as in 1956; All Spring
Wheat Down 10 Percent

The 1957 wheat production, based on conditions June 1, is forecast at
971 million bushels. A crop of this size would be 3 percent less than the
1956 production of 997 million bushels and 14 percent less than the 1946-55
average of 1,131 million bushels. For all wheat, the indicated yield per
seeded acre is 19.6 bushels compared with 16.4 bushels last year and 15.3
bushels for the 10-year average.

The winter wheat crop is estimated at 736 million bushels. This is an
increase of 33 million bushels from the May 1 forecast and compares with
735 million bushels produced in 1956 and the average of 862 million bushels.
Increases from May 1 prospects, largely in Kansas, Nebraska and Colorado, more
than offset decreases in several south central and southwestern States.

The indicated yield at 23.6 bushels per acre for harvest on June 1 is
the highest of record, sharply above the 1956 yield of 20.6 bushels and the
average of 18.6 bushels. Yield prospects were uniformly good throughout the
winter wheat producing area. Most States except Utah expect above average
yields, and New York, New Jersey, Indiana, Maryland, West Virginia and Arizona
expect record yields. Adequate to excessive moisture during May throughout
the winter wheat producing areas was mostly beneficial and losses were
moderate.

Production of spring wheat other than durum was indicated to be
205 million bushels, 18 million less than the 1956 crop and 34 million bushels
below average. Moisture conditions during May generally favored germination
and early development in all major producing States. Precipitation was
normal or above during the first three weeks of May followed by dry, warm
weather. Plant diseases and insect pests threatened crops in North and South
Dakota, and eastern Montana. The acreage seeded in Idaho is indicated to be
larger than expected on March 1; however, seedings in Minnesota may be
slightly lower.

A durum wheat crop of about 30 million bushels was indicated for the
Dakotas, Montana and Minnesota. This compares with last year's production of
40 million bushels and equals the average production. Durum growers in the
Dakotas and Montana apparently seeded their intended acreage, but seedings in
Minnesota were much above intentions due mostly to changes in wheat allotment
legislation. In Montana, moisture was adequate and the crop had a good start,
except for some acreage in the north central section. Much of the acreage in
North Dakota, the leading durum wheat State, was seeded with rust resistant
varieties; as of June 1 there was no evidence of rust, which had caused heavy
damage to durum in the Dakotas and Minnesota for several years prior to 1956.

U. S. Wheat and Flour Exports
Exceed Record of 1948-49

United States wheat and flour exports during July-April 1956-57 were 448 million bushels, according to the Bureau of the Census. Inspections of wheat for export during May bring total exports (with an allowance for flour) for the 11-month period July-May to about 495 million bushels. If the rate of exports during June should continue at approximately the same rate as for the past 11 months, total exports for the crop year July 1956-June 1957 would reach about 535 million bushels. This would be 31 million bushels higher than the record of 504 million bushels in 1948-49.

Bureau of the Census data showing actual destinations of exports during this 11-month period are not yet available. Indications are that the quantities taken by the major importing countries, in millions of bushels, compared with exports to the same markets during the corresponding period a year ago (shown in parentheses) were as follows: India, 53.6 (43.6); Japan, 46.2 (37.9); United Kingdom, 36.7 (20.0); West Germany, 33.7 (15.8); Yugoslavia, 32.4 (35.5); Pakistan, 22.1 (4.6); Netherlands, 19.4 (20.8); Greece, 18.7 (11.8); Belgium-Luxembourg, 17.3 (4.9) and Turkey, 16.9 (4.0).

Prospective Supplies
by Classes Are Ample
to Very Large

Analysis of prospective supply and distribution by classes indicates continued very large supplies of hard red winter wheat and abundant supplies of hard red spring wheat. Supplies of durum should more than meet domestic requirements, with prospects for a durum crop of about 30 million bushels. Prospective supplies of soft red winter wheat are ample to provide for sizable exports in addition to meeting domestic needs.

Minimum 1957 Terminal and
County Wheat Price-Support
Rates Announced

The U. S. Department of Agriculture on May 16 announced minimum 1957-crop wheat price-support rates for terminals and for 2,694 commercial and 378 noncommercial wheat producing counties.

County rates, which range from $2.29 to 98 cents (noncommercial) per bushel depending upon location, are further adjusted up or down for grade and quality to determine support prices.

The county rates and the support rates for the 1957 crop were based on the minimum national average support price of $2.00 per bushel announced July 2, 1956.

Table 3 .- Wheat and flour: U.S. exports by country of destination,
July-April 1955-56 and 1956-57 1/

Continent and country	July-April 1955-56			July-April 1956-57		
	Wheat	Flour 2/	Total	Wheat	Flour 2/	Total
	(Thousands of bushels, grain equivalent)					
Western Hemisphere:						
Canada	1,573	214	1,787	97	156	253
Mexico	3,919	15	3,934	71	14	85
Central America	687	3,258	3,945	1,131	3,653	4,784
Cuba	1,667	2,912	4,579	2,720	3,393	6,113
British West Indies	-	1,998	1,998	2	2,874	2,876
Colombia	2,072	87	2,159	2,624	96	2,720
Venezuela	83	3,973	4,056	354	5,381	5,735
Peru	3,304	186	3,490	3,347	241	3,588
Bolivia	1,585	949	2,534	2,771	1,285	4,056
Chile	1,388	4	1,392	4,883	47	4,930
Brazil	13,911	885	14,796	6,738	16	6,754
Paraguay	-		-	706	297	1,003
Others	605	2,753	3,358	826	2,987	3,813
Total	30,794	17,234	48,028	26,270	20,440	46,710
Europe:						
Norway	1,587	1,112	2,699	1,889	792	2,681
Denmark	244	8	252	3,456	34	3,490
United Kingdom	15,098	1,069	16,167	31,806	1,538	33,344
Netherlands	14,986	3,073	18,059	16,486	2,867	19,353
Belgium-Luxembourg	4,182	18	4,200	17,321	21	17,342
France	3/	3/	3/	30,895	13	30,908
West Germany	11,745	1	11,746	31,668	321	31,989
Austria	403	-	403	1,870	23	1,893
Switzerland	190	-	190	8,274	6	8,280
Finland	251	-	251	2,979	-	2,979
Portugal	1,939	151	2,090	5,574	206	5,780
Italy	2,925	983	3,908	9,295	2,223	11,518
Yugoslavia	29,963	9	29,972	24,432	535	24,967
Greece	11,014	3	11,017	17,863	432	18,295
Others	2,018	37	2,055	2,082	158	2,240
Total	96,545	6,464	103,009	205,890	9,169	215,059
Asia and Oceania:						
Turkey	2,571	-	2,571	16,879	-	16,879
Israel	6,623	8	6,631	7,358	596	7,954
Saudi Arabia	294	1,689	1,983	977	3,017	3,994
India	3,405	39	3,444	43,580	53	43,633
Pakistan	4,537	-	4,537	21,970	113	22,083
Indochina	-	1,299	1,299	-	2,908	2,908
Indonesia	-	421	421	-	4,003	4,003
Philippines	-	4,052	4,052	-	5,365	5,365
Korea	4,077	-	4,077	11,980	985	12,965
Taiwan	5,792	6	5,798	5,485	448	5,933
Japan	32,577	1,020	33,597	39,719	1,974	41,693
Other Asia	213	3,612	3,825	2,099	2,963	5,062
Oceania	-	23	23	14	209	223
Total	60,089	12,169	72,258	150,061	22,634	172,695
Africa:						
Tunisia	359	-	359	2,933	30	2,963
Egypt	14,121	634	14,755	1,071	360	1,431
Canary Islands	1,849	-	1,849	165	-	165
French West Africa	-	10	10	2,353	7	2,360
British West Africa	-	2,094	2,094	-	3,134	3,134
Others	2,091	1,510	3,601	1,628	1,855	3,483
Total	18,420	4,248	22,668	8,150	5,386	13,536
Unspecified	1,816	747	2,563	1	39	40
World total	207,664	40,862	248,526	390,372	57,668	448,040

1/ Includes exports for relief or charity which are not included in the Census figures.
2/ Wholly of U.S. wheat.
3/ Less than 500 bushels.

The Department also announced a list of premiums and discounts for different classes and qualities of wheat. In general, terminal rates and basic county rates are for Grade No. 1 wheat. Premiums and discounts are applied to basic rates to determine the support price for individual lots of wheat which are of other grade or have other quality factors.

Location differentials used in the 1957-crop rates are generally in line with those used in prior years except for changes due to freight increases. The relationships between terminals are based principally on average differences in cash market prices. For major producing areas, the county rates reflect these terminal rates less the freight and handling charges needed to get the wheat to terminal markets. The support rates in counties farthest from terminals are generally the lowest, reflecting the higher freight costs.

The discount schedule for 1957 wheat includes a 2-cents-per-bushel discount for hard yellow wheat (produced mostly in Midwest) because this subclass of hard red winter is not considered to be as high in quality for milling and baking purposes as other wheats of this class. No change is made in the 2-cents-per-bushel discount for red and white (except Baart and Bluestem) wheats in the west. The red durum discount continues at 20 cents per bushel. Mixed wheat will be discounted ranging from 2 to 15 cents per bushel depending upon the mixture. Discounts are unchanged for grades below No. 1, or garlicky or smutty wheats.

The discount of 20 cents per bushel for undesirable varieties of wheat, because of inferior milling or baking qualities, continues under the 1957 wheat support program. 2/ Production of these varieties is declining rapidly.

No change is being made in the premiums for protein and for No. 1 heavy hard red spring wheat. Because higher market prices for durum are moving back toward their historical relationship with other wheats, the premium for hard amber durum is reduced to 15 cents per bushel from the 25 cent premium of the last two years and the amber durum premium is reduced from 15 to 10 cents per bushel.

Representative Support Prices
by Classes and Grades

There are wide differences in the grades and classes of wheat most commonly produced and marketed in the various wheat areas of the U. S. In some areas, No. 1 grade hard wheat predominates. In other areas, grades No. 2 or No. 3 soft red winter wheat predominates. In the Pacific Northwest No. 1 soft white predominates. Table 4 shows specific support rates in 1956 and 1957 for representative classes and grades of wheat produced in the different areas, with storage paid at the listed terminals. In these examples, premiums

2/ The 23 varieties on which discounts apply were listed in The Wheat Situation, April 1957, page 19.

and discounts were applied to basic rates to obtain the support rate for
individual kinds of wheat listed.

Table 4.- Wheat: Representative support prices, by classes and grades,
terminal markets, 1956 and 1957

| Class, grade and terminal | Support rate per bushel | |
	1956	1957
	Dollars	Dollars
Hard Red Sping		
Grade No. 1 Heavy, 16 percent protein, Minneapolis	2.43	2.45
Grade No. 1 Heavy, 14 percent protein, Minneapolis	2.39	2.41
Grade No. 1, ordinary protein, Minneapolis	2.34	2.36
Soft Red Winter		
Grade No. 2 garlicky, Baltimore	2.27	2.28
Grade No. 2 St. Louis, Chicago	2.30	2.31
Grade No. 2 light garlicky, Chicago	2.24	2.25
Grade No. 2 Kansas City	2.30	2.31
Hard Red Winter		
Grade No. 2, Chicago	2.30	2.31
Grade No. 2, Kansas City	2.30	2.31
Grade No. 2, Galveston	2.45	2.48
Soft White		
Grade No. 1, Portland	2.21	2.22
Grade No. 1, San Francisco	2.29	2.30
Hard White - Baart and Bluestem		
Grade No. 1, Portland	2.23	2.24
Durum		
Grade No. 1, Amber, Minneapolis	2.49	2.46
Grade No. 1, Hard Amber, Minneapolis	2.59	2.51

In order for a producer in commercial wheat-producing States to get
wheat price support in 1957, he must be in compliance with his 1957 wheat
acreage allotment and be eligible to receive a wheat marketing card on all
other farms in the county in which he has an interest.

In the 12 States designated as the noncommercial wheat producing
area, farm wheat allotments and marketing quotas do not apply and the support
rates are lower than in the other 36 States. 3/

3/ Rates in the noncommercial area are 75 percent of the rates determined
on the basis of the $2.00 per bushel national average support price. The
States included in the noncommercial area are: Alabama, Arizona, Connecticut,
Florida, Louisiana, Maine, Massachusetts, Mississippi, Nevada, New Hampshire,
Rhode Island and Vermont.

Table 5 .-- Wheat and rye: Cash closing prices and support prices at terminal markets, specified months and days, 1956 and 1957 1/

Commodity, market and grade	Cash closing prices								1956-crop support prices	
	Monthly average					June 20, 1956	Daily range		Effective June 20, 1957	Terminal
	May 1956	Feb. 1957	Mar. 1957	Apr. 1957	May 1957		June 13, 1957	June 20, 1957		
	Dol.	Dol.	Dol.	Dol.	Dol.	Dol.	Dol.	Dol.	Dol.	Dol.
Wheat:										
Chicago:										
No. 2 Hard Red Winter	2.24	2.35	2.28	2.25	2.18	2.13	---	2.07	2.30	2.30
No. 2 Soft Red Winter	2.24	2.36	2.28	2.23	2.14	2.16	2.05	2.05	2.30	2.30
St. Louis:										
No. 2 Soft Red Winter	2.23	2.33	2.31	2.25	2.18	2.15-2.17	2.08	2.03-2.06	2.30	2.30
Kansas City:										
No. 2 Hard Red Winter, ordinary protein	2.23	2.32	2.32	2.30	2.16	2.08-2.10	2.22-2.23	2.16-2.18	2.30	2.30
No. 2 Hrd Red Winter, 13 percent protein	2.31	2.33	2.34	2.33	2.23	2.09-2.31	2.23-2.29	2.17-2.32	2.32	2.32
No. 2 Soft Red Winter	2.20	2.34	2.33	2.29	2.18	2.08-2.10	2.18-2.19	2.13-2.16	2.30	2.30
Fort Worth:										
No. 2 Hard Red Winter	2.42	2.51	2.53	2.47	2.39	2.27-2.34	2.29-2.38	2.29-2.38	2/2.45	2/2.45
Minneapolis:										
No. 1 Dark Northern Spring, ordinary protein	2.32	2.33	2.31	2.30	2.24	2.27-2.30	2.23-2.24	2.25-2.26	2.34	2.34
No. 1 Dark Northern Spring, 13 percent protein	2.37	2.35	2.33	2.32	2.27	2.31-2.36	2.27-2.29	2.28-2.31	2.37	2.37
No. 1 Dark Northern Spring, 15 percent protein	2.43	2.39	2.40	2.40	2.36	2.38-2.43	2.38-2.43	2.43-2.48	2.40	2.40
No. 2 Hard Amber Durum	2.70	2.66	2.64	2.59	2.52	2.56-2.63	2.48-2.52	2.46-2.50	2.58	2.58
Portland:										
No. 1 Hard White, 12 percent protein	2.52	2.59	2.62	2.63	2.59	2.52-2.53	2.48-2.52	2.48-2.50	3/2.26	3/2.26
No. 1 Soft White	2.22	2.59	2.62	2.63	2.59	2.09-2.11	2.48-2.52	2.48-2.50	2.21	2.21
Toledo:										
No. 2 Soft Red Winter	2.16	2.24	2.18	2.16	2.05	2.22-2.23	2.00-2.01	2.00-2.01	---	---
No. 2 Soft White	2.17	2.22	2.17	2.16	2.04	2.24-2.25	2.01-2.02	2.00-2.01	---	---
Rye:										
Minneapolis, No..2	1.22	1.38	1.38	1.35	1.23	1.18-1.21	1.26-1.31	1.30-1.35	1.50	1.50

1/ Cash grain closing prices are not the range of cash sales during the day but are on-track cash prices established at the close of the market. The terminal rate is a rate used in determining the effective support price for grain in terminal storage or in transit to terminal and for calculating most county price support rates. The effective support price is the established terminal support rate for grain received by rail minus the deduction for storage as of the date shown. A comparison of the above effective price support rate and the current cash closing price is an indication of whether the market price is above or below the support rate provided the location of the grain is on track at the specified terminals. The monthly average price is the simple average of the daily closing prices.

2/ Galveston effective and terminal support price. The cash price at Fort Worth is usually backed by paid-in freight which will carry it to Galveston. Therefore cash prices at Fort Worth may usually be compared with the effective support price at Galveston. A terminal support price is not established for Fort Worth.

3/ Applies only to the varieties Baart and Bluestem of the sub-class Hard White.

Table 6 .- Wheat, 1956 crop: Quantities repaid and delivered under loans, and delivered under purchase agreements, through May 15, 1957, by States

State	Warehouse and farm loans			Purchase agreements		
	Total under loans	Repaid	Delivered	Total under purchase agreements	Elected to be delivered	Delivered
	1,000 bu.	1,000 bu.	1,000 bu.	1,000 bu.	1,000 bu.	1,000 bu.
Alabama	7	7	---	---	---	---
Arizona	117	117	---	---	---	---
Arkansas	545	434	106	5	---	---
California	1,570	1,496	65	22	3	2
Colorado	2,720	769	1,590	195	60	27
Delaware	22	13	9	---	---	---
Georgia	579	253	326	2	---	---
Idaho	9,941	9,574	3	41	---	---
Illinois	7,099	5,037	1,907	79	69	12
Indiana	1,257	763	386	20	10	1/
Iowa	667	28	621	19	2	---
Kansas	69,152	3,372	64,001	2,262	1,091	1,148
Kentucky	1,023	366	655	---	---	---
Maryland	256	208	48	---	---	---
Michigan	1,176	847	260	73	17	1
Minnesota	3,344	805	1,190	684	322	63
Missouri	9,858	2,289	7,145	43	12	11
Montana	13,725	9,517	829	3,884	2,517	185
Nebraska	11,284	2,491	7,890	519	287	132
Nevada	5	4	1	---	---	---
New Jersey	77	47	18	---	---	---
New Mexico	447	362	82	---	---	---
New York	604	238	251	27	15	6
North Carolina	386	259	110	4	---	---
North Dakota	29,221	5,875	11,823	9,493	6,711	1,171
Ohio	2,507	1,371	1,082	49	5	2
Oklahoma	24,394	15,533	8,817	96	38	5
Oregon	7,980	7,944	18	35	---	---
Pennsylvania	341	233	96	5	---	1
South Carolina	211	87	125	1	---	---
South Dakota	3,739	576	1,700	728	556	82
Tennessee	462	153	307	2	2	1
Texas	7,560	3,107	4,445	24	7	7
Utah	747	744	---	1	---	---
Virginia	820	710	111	2	---	---
Washington	19,252	19,197	8	81	---	---
West Virginia	1	1	1/	---	---	---
Wisconsin	7	1	---	1/	1/	---
Wyoming	446	126	105	70	40	30
Total U. S.	233,549	94,954	116,130	18,466	11,764	2,886

1/ Less than 500 bushels.

Commodity Stabilization Service, U.S.D.A.

Price Support Program
  Similar to Past Year

        The 1957 wheat crop will be supported as in the past through loans on
farm- and warehouse-stored wheat and through the purchase of wheat delivered
by producers under purchase agreements. Loans and purchase agreements will be
available from harvest time through January 31, 1958. In most States, loans
will mature on March 31, 1958 and in some eastern and southern States the
date of maturity will be February 28, 1958. Loans will be available from
County Agricultural Stabilization and Conservation offices and eligible
lending institutions.

Cash Wheat Prices
  Adjusting Downward
  Seasonally

        Cash prices have been adjusting downward seasonally, though delayed
combining and some concern over damage of wet fields in the Southwest have
resulted in temporary increases. Compared with the high levels reached in
April, prices on June 24 were as follows: $2.20 for No. 2 Hard Winter at
Kansas City, down 13 cents; $2.29 for No. 1 Dark Northern Spring at Minneap-
olis, down 3 cents; $2.06 for No. 2 Soft Red Winter at St. Louis, down 23 cents
and $2.49 for No. 1 Soft White at Portland, down 15 cents.

        As of May 31, 94.5 million bushels of the 233.7 million of 1956-crop
wheat placed under loan were redeemed and 120.7 delivered to the CCC. Producers delivered 3.5 million bushels of wheat under purchase agreements by the
end of May. There were originally 18.5 million under purchase agreements, of
which farmers had elected to deliver 11.8 million bushels. Extended 1956-crop
loans for another year were made on 1.8 million bushels.

1957-58 Price to Growers
  May Again Average Near
  $2.00 Support Level

        The U. S. average price to growers, which includes unredeemed loan
wheat at the support rate, may again average near the national support level
of $2.00 per bushel.

        The price to growers in 1955-56 averaged $1.99, which was 9 cents
under the national average support rate. In 1956-57 the average is expected to
be about 3 cents below the announced rate of $2.00. This improved relationship
reflects the generally higher prices received under the new export program.
The extent to which Southwest wheat is of high moisture content will be a
factor in determining how near to the $2.00 support level prices will average
in 1957-58. Moisture content of winter wheat may be high enough so that
substantial quantities will not qualify for CCC farm storage loans. The result would be an increase in cash sales following harvest and weakening of
prices.

Since support programs were inaugurated in 1938, support prices in the past have declined in only 3 years--from 1948 to 1949, when the national average rate to growers dropped from $2.00 to $1.95; from $2.24 in 1954 to $2.08 in 1955 and from $2.08 in 1955 to $2.00 in 1956. 4/ The decline from 1957 to 1958 is from $2.00 to $1.78 the national average minimum announced for 1958.

Table 7 shows the relationship of monthly average prices at Kansas City and the support rate at that market. On the basis of changes in carryover and size of exports, there appears to be a greater similarity between the situation in 1957-58 and 1955-56 than for 1948-49 and 1954-55. If 1955-56 is indicative of what may be expected in 1957-58, the low market average price would come in August and the high in April. In 1948, the low was also in August, but in 1954 it was in June. Because of the late harvest this year, a low average price in June is not likely. The high monthly average in 1954-55 occurred in May, and while the high month in 1948-49 was in December, April was only 2.7 cents lower.

Table 7.--Wheat, No 2 Hard Winter: Price and support rate relationships and related factors, 3 years of declining support rates

Item	1948-49	1954-55	1955-56	1957-58
	Cents	Cents	Cents	Cents
No. 2 H. W., Kansas City:				
Gross Loan	223.0	253.0	237.0	231.0
Price 1/				
High month average	228.7(Dec.'48)	253.1(May'55)	233.3(Apr.'56)	---
Low month average	215.0(Aug.'48)	215.3(June'54)	215.1(Aug.'55)	3/(219.0)
Price advance	13.7	37.8	18.2	
High month average above loan	5.7	.1	-3.7	---
Low month average below loan	8.0	37.7	21.9	3/ (12.0)
Annual weighted price	218.8	237.2	217.7	---
	Mil.bu.	Mil. bu.	Mil. bu.	Mil. bu.
Supply and distribution factors (All classes)				
Carryover change	+111.4	+102.7	-2.8	-23.0
Net exports	502.5	270.2	336.2	395.0

1/ Cash prices computed by weighting selling price by number of carlots sold, as reported in the Kansas City Grain Market Review. 2/ April 1949 was $2.26 per bushel. 3/ Price as of June 3, the low between June 1 and 24, 1957.

_____

4/ These changes are the result of (1) changes in the support price as a percentage of parity, and (2) changes in parity price itself (See The Wheat Situation, April 1957, page 23, footnote 10).

The price of wheat at Kansas City again is expected to average lower relative to the loan than the national average because of heavy early season sales. The weighted price of No. 2 Hard Red Winter at that market was below the support price by 4.2 cents in 1948-49, 15.8 cents in 1954-55, and 19.3 cents in 1955-56.

Preliminary Tally in Wheat Referendum Shows 83.3 Percent Favorable

Preliminary returns from the referendum held on June 20 in the 36-State wheat producing area show that 83.3 percent of farmers voting favored marketing quotas for the 1958-crop wheat.

Incomplete returns show a total of 172,216 votes counted--about 38.6 percent less than last year. Of these 143,333 (83.3 percent) favored quotas on 1958-crop wheat and 28,883 (16.7 percent) were opposed.

Marketing quotas will be in effect for the 1958 crop because of approval by two-thirds or more of farmers voting in the referendum.

The referendum this year marked the seventh time farmers have voted on marketing quotas for wheat. They approved quotas for the 1941 crop by an 81.0 percent favorable vote, for the 1942 crop by 82.4 percent, the 1954 crop by 87.2 percent, the 1955 crop by 73.3 percent, the 1956 crop by 77.5 percent and the 1957 crop by 87.4 percent.

With the approval of quotas, producers in commercial wheat States who stay within the acreage allotted for their farms will be eligible for the full level of price support. In the noncommercial States 5/ the wheat price support will be at 75 percent of the level calculated on the national average.

Marketing quota penalties, equal to 45 percent of the wheat parity price as of May 1, 1958, will be assessed against the farm marketing excess. The marketing quota penalty rate on "excess" wheat of the 1957 crop was set at $1.12 per bushel, which was 45 percent of the parity price of $2.50 per bushel.

1957-Crop Soil Bank Certificate Redemption Plans

Plans for exchanging grains in the CCC-owned inventory for Soil Bank certificates earned by farmers who reduced 1957 acreages of wheat, corn and rice were announced on May 23. The certificates are also redeemable in cash.

Under the 1956 Acreage Reserve Program, participating grain farmers could exchange their Acreage Reserve certificates at 105 percent of face value for the grain for which they put acreage under the Program, or for other grains held by CCC such as barley, rye, oats and grain sorghums.

5/ States included in the noncommercial area are listed on page 12, footnote 3.

This 5 percent premium, applied in a different manner, also will be in effect this year on all grains except wheat. That is, a wheat farmer who participates in the Acreage Reserve can redeem his certificates for barley, rye, oats or grain sorghums at 5 percent below the current support price, for these grains. However, certificates can be exchanged for wheat only at the current support rate. A wheat certificate may not be exchanged for corn or rice; the regulation in this respect being the same as under the 1956 Program.

The value of wheat offered in exchange for certificates has been set at the 1957 support rate rather than at support less 5 percent, to minimize the possibility of impairing the market price for the grain--which would conflict with the provisions of the Soil Bank Act. In contrast with most feed grains used mainly for direct livestock feeding, most wheat when redeemed could be expected to flow directly into market channels. The volume of wheat redemptions which could result this year might also adversely affect the wheat export program, which is designed to strengthen prices by drawing wheat export requirements from normal channels of trade rather than from CCC stocks.

CCC-owned grain for redemption of Soil Bank certificates will be delivered at local warehouses, terminal elevators, or from CCC binsites depending upon its availability and the wishes of producers. Redemptions may be limited to certain grains and within certain areas if conditions require.

Provision is also being made to enable producers to obtain their own farm-stored or warehouse-stored grain, which is still under price-support loan, at the same price they would pay for CCC-owned grain at a binsite or warehouse. Delivery in these instances would be at the point of storage. Even if the grain is from a previous crop year under farm storage reseal loan, when support rates were higher, the purchase price to the producer will be based on current support rates. Storage payments will be made by CCC on resealed or extended reseal loans for the actual period of the loan. Certificates may be used for purchasing part or all of grain under loan, or under reseal or extended reseal loans.

Grains will not be available for redemption during harvest periods which are established for each area--that is, CCC will not exchange a particular grain for certificates until after the 1957 harvest season for that grain in the area. This harvesting limitation will also apply to purchases of grain under loan by use of certificates. This provision is designated to furnish maximum protection to prices during heavy marketing periods.

Certificates exchanged for a specific grain must be used before the beginning of the 1958-crop marketing year for that grain.

Last year, when farmers who placed wheat acreage under the Program could exchange their certificates at 105 percent of the face value for that grain, they purchased a little under 900,000 bushels and redeemed price support loans on nearly 19,500 bushels more.

THE WORLD WHEAT SITUATION

World Wheat Trade in 1956-57
 May Exceed 1.2 Billion
Bushels, a New Record

          Preliminary data indicate that world wheat exports in 1956-57 will
exceed the previous record by a substantial margin, according to the Foreign
Agricultural Service. The 1956-57 estimate of 1,210 million bushels exceeds
the former record of 1,066 million bushels in 1951-52 by more than 13 percent.
Exports at this level will be 17 percent above 1955-56 and 29 percent above
the 10-year 1946-55 average of 941 million bushels.

          Some of the more important factors causing this increase in the world
wheat trade are decreased domestic supplies in Europe, caused by the serious
crop damage in the winter of 1955-56; increased exports from the United States
exported under special export Programs such a Public Law 480 and some increases in wheat consumption in various countries such as Japan.

          The larger wheat exports indicated for 1956-57 reflect much larger
exports from the United States, substantial increases from Australia but
decreases in exports from Canada and Argentina.

          Preliminary estimates of world exports in 1956-57 compared with
exports in 1955-56 in parenthesis, include, in million bushels: United
States, 535 (346); Canada, 270 (289); Australia, 125 (102) and Argentina, 95
(115). Estimated exports from other countries total 185 million bushels.
The Soviet Union is expected to export a large share of this amount, with
small exporters moving minor quantities.

Four Exporting-Country Supplies
  Down from Year Ago

          June 1 world wheat supplies for export and carryover in the four major
exporting countries (United States, Canada, Argentina and Australia) totaled
1,853 million bushels--83 million less than a year earlier and 50 million
less than 2 years ago (table 8). United States supplies, at 940 million
bushels, were 136 million below a year ago while Canadian supplies at 705 mil-
lion-- an all-time record high for that date--were 90 million larger. Supplies in Australia totaled 91 million--a drop of 69 million while supplies in
Argentina increased 32 million bushels to 117 million bushels on June 1.
From July through May, United States exports amounted to about 595 million
bushels--200 million more than in the previous year. From August through
May, Canada exported about 214 million, 21 million less than last year. From
December through May, Argentina exported about 54 million, 1 million less
than a year earlier and in the same period Australia exported 55 million, the
same as a year ago.

Table 8 .- Wheat: Supplies available for export and carryover in the United States, Canada, Argentina and Australia, June 1, 1955-57

Carryover stocks, July 1
New crop
   Total supplies
Domestic requirements for season 2/
Supplies available for export and carryover
Exports, July 1 through May 31 3/
Supplies on June 1 for export and carryover 4/

Carryover stocks, August 1
New crop
   Total supplies
Domestic requirements for season 2/
Supplies available for export and carryover
Exports, August 1 through May 31 3/
Supplies on June 1 for export and carryover

Carryover stocks, December 1			
New crop			
Total supplies	3 3	27	307
Domestic requirements for season 2/	129	136	136
Supplies available for export and carryover	214	140	171
Exports, December 1 through May 31 3/	67	55	54
Supplies on June 1 for export and carryover	147	85	117

AUSTRALIA

Carryover stocks, December 1	93	92	84
New crop	169	195	135
Total supplies	262	287	219
Domestic requirements for season 2/	72	72	73
Supplies available for export and carryover	190	215	146
Exports, December 1 through May 31 3/	55	55	55
Supplies on June 1 for export and carryover	135	160	91

TOTALS FOR THE FOUR COUNTRIES

Carryover stocks, beginning of the season	1,688	1,711	1,703
New crop	1,745	1,817	1,932
Total supplies	3,433	3,528	3,635
Domestic requirements for season 2/	951	952	964
Supplies available for export and carryover	2,482	2,576	2,671
Exports, season through May 31 3/	579	640	818
Supplies on June 1 for export and carryover	1,903	1,936	·1,853

1/ Preliminary.
2/ Estimated requirements for seed, food (milling for domestic use), and feed for the season.
3/ Exports of wheat and flour in grain equivalent.
4/ Without imports

Crop Prospects Favorable
 In Most Northern
 Hemisphere Countries

      The outlook for the 1957 wheat crop in Northern Hemisphere countries is generally favorable, on the basis of preliminary indications available to the Foreign Agricultural Service. Better prospects are reported for most parts of Europe and also for the countries of Asia for which reports are available. Total wheat production in the United States, as already pointed out, is expected to be about 3 percent less than the 1956 harvest. Seeding has been completed only a short time in Canada and no official estimate of the area sown to wheat will be available until August 9.

      On the basis of Canadian farmers' intentions to plant as of March 1, total wheat acreage in that country will be 1.4 million acres less than in 1956. Reports in mid-June stated that rain was needed to prevent deterioration of the crop over wide areas of the wheat belt. Specific areas mentioned as needing rain were western Saskatchewan, eastern Alberta, and the Peace River area. Damage to winter wheat was relatively light this year, only 4 percent compared with winterkill of 11 percent a year ago. Winter wheat in Canada is normally only about 5 percent of total wheat production. Mexico's wheat production is at an all-time high. The current estimates of 44 million bushels exceeds the previous record in 1956 by 9 percent. Both acreage and yields are larger than in 1956.

      The outlook for wheat in Europe is generally promising, and a somewhat larger crop than in 1956 now seems assured despite dry conditions reported in a number of areas. Increased production will be especially marked in France, where very heavy winterkill reduced the outturn sharply last year. Other Western European countries reporting better prospects for this year's crop include Yugoslavia, Italy and Portugal.

      Prospects for other Danube Basin countries and Central Europe are also somewhat better than at this time last year. The 1956 outturn in that area was somewhat below average.

      On the basis of preliminary reports, the wheat harvest recently completed in India and Pakistan was larger than in 1956. The crop in India is now placed at 321 million bushels, second only to the previous record 1954 production and 50 percent above the 1945-49 average. A larger wheat acreage accounts for the near-record outturn. Pakistan's current harvest is estimated to be about 135 million bushels, about the same as in 1954. Both acreage and yields are larger than in 1956.

      Preliminary estimates place Japan's production at about 46.5 million bushels. This is smaller than the crops of the past 3 years and is somewhat less than had been expected earlier in the season. The reduction is attributed to drought. In Turkey also, drought is a factor in current prospects. Drought for a second year in the important producing Anatolian Plateau makes the outlook there uncertain. Wheat development is about 3 weeks later than usual, and the extent of rainfall during the remainder of the season will determine the final outcome.

Canada Makes Final Payment for
1955-Crop; Announces Initial
Payment for 1957

The Canadian Wheat Board on May 22 began mailing final payment checks to farmers for their 1955 wheat delivered to elevators. Prices received by farmers for respective grades of 1955 crop were lower than in the previous year. The final payment for No. 1 Manitoba delivered at the Lakehead brought the price to $1.607 per bushel, compared with $1.648 for the 1954 crop. Fina prices paid for other grades were also lower than the previous year. The low prices for the 1955 crop were based on (1)somewhat lower transfer price of th unsold wheat to the new account, and (2) somewhat lower prices realized from sales during the past year.

Initial payments on the 1957 wheat crop were announced on May 3 at $1.40 a bushel for No. 1 Northern Wheat, based upon delivery at the Lakehead. The initial payment on wheat has been the same since 1950.

Upon delivery of his grain to the local elevator, the farmer receives the initial payment less transportation to the Lakehead and other marketing costs. A final payment is made to the farmer after the Wheat Board completes marketings of the grain crop and after total costs are deducted.

Canada Increases Grain
Storage Space

Total licensed grain storage capacity in Canada on March 31, 1957, was 627.4 million bushels, according to records of the Board of Grain Commissioner for Canada. This indicates a gain of 3 percent over the capacity a year earlier, when the total licensed capacity was reported at 609 million bushels.

Licensed storage space is now available for about 612.2 million bushels in elevators, including permanent and temporary annexes. The remaining space, for 15.2 million bushels, is in public country supplementary storage, under temporary license. Though considered suitable for emergency storing of grain, this space cannot qualify for licensing under the provisions of the Canada Grain Act of September 26, 1951. Unlicensed off-farm storage for 0.9 million bushels is also available. About 85 percent of the total licensed storage is located in the Western Division. The greatest amount of storage is in Saskatchewan, with total space for 211.6 million bushels. Alberta, with space for 140.6 million bushels, is the second largest storage area.

Grain supplies in Canada are at an all-time high. When last reported, as of March 31, 1957, wheat supplies in all positions were 831 million bushels well above the previous record of 762 million at the end of March 1943, and the 1947-56 average of 454 million. Stocks of coarse grains were also very large, though not an all-time record. With total grain stocks at their peak, stocks of wheat remaining on farms were at a new high. Coarse grain stocks still on farms were large, but below their record.

Table 9 .- Wheat, No. 2 Hard Winter: Weighted average cash price per bushel, by months, and loan rate, Kansas City, 1937-57 1/

Year beginning July	July	Aug.	Sept.	Oct.	Nov.	Dec.	Jan.	Feb.	Mar.	Apr.	May	June	Loan rate at Kansas City 2/
	Cents	Cents	Cents	Cents	Cents	Cents	Cents	Cents	Cents	Cents	Cents	Cents	Cents
1937	122.5	111.8	109.5	106.0	94.2	96.5	102.7	99.6	91.5	84.6	79.7	76.7	---
1938	70.0	65.5	65.7	64.7	63.3	66.2	70.9	69.2	68.7	69.6	75.7	70.9	72
1939	66.7	64.6	85.9	82.7	85.8	98.3	101.2	99.4	102.1	105.7	94.7	76.3	77
1940	70.7	69.3	75.8	81.6	84.5	83.0	84.7	77.8	85.1	87.2	90.4	97.3	77
1941	98.3	106.6	114.1	112.2	113.4	120.1	125.6	123.1	121.0	114.6	114.9	110.9	110
1942	107.9	111.2	120.3	120.5	123.1	130.5	136.8	137.0	139.9	138.4	138.1	137.0	127
1943	140.1	139.8	145.8	152.3	156.4	162.3	164.8	163.0	165.2	164.0	163.2	155.6	137
1944	152.1	150.8	153.0	161.3	159.1	162.0	163.6	165.8	166.3	165.7	166.7	168.2	150
1945	158.3	159.8	162.1	168.3	168.9	169.2	169.2	169.1	172.1	172.1	186.1	186.1	153
1946	197.8	193.8	196.0	203.9	210.4	207.2	209.0	226.1	269.4	267.6	269.3	237.3	164
1947	228.8	231.8	261.6	295.3	299.9	301.1	303.2	250.8	215.4	244.5	240.2	229.4	202
1948	219.3	215.0	220.4	222.6	228.2	228.7	225.0	219.6	224.1	226.0	222.1	195.1	223
1949	200.4	206.0	215.2	218.8	220.2	222.1	222.3	222.4	227.2	230.6	230.0	217.0	220
1950	222.8	220.9	221.0	217.9	222.4	234.6	240.2	247.6	240.1	243.5	238.4	234.4	225
1951	230.7	233.0	238.3	245.2	254.0	254.1	251.9	249.2	249.6	249.2	244.6	230.6	244
1952	225.1	232.3	240.9	241.6	245.8	244.5	240.2	235.8	239.5	238.7	235.5	203.6	248
1953	208.6	217.5	221.7	228.8	233.7	237.5	237.9	239.3	241.7	244.7	237.0	215.3	249
1954	232.4	235.2	238.9	241.1	243.9	245.5	244.3	245.5	245.6	246.1	253.1	219.0	253
1955	216.0	215.1	215.5	219.8	220.7	225.3	224.2	221.6	228.5	233.3	224.2	210.0	237
1956	208.7	219.0	228.2	231.0	235.8	234.3	235.8	233.8	233.5	230.2	223.1		230
1957													3/231

1/ Cash prices computed by weighting selling price by number of carlots sold, as reported in the Kansas City Grain Market Review. In this price, wheat of above as well as below 13 percent protein is included.

2/ Loan rate is for wheat of less than 13 percent. Ceiling became effective January 4, 1944 at $1.62 includ-ing 1½ cents commission, basis protein of less than 13 percent. On December 13, 1944 it was raised to $1.66, on May 30, 1945 to $1.691, on March 4, 1946 to $1.721 and on May 13, 1946 to $1.871. On June 30, 1946, ceilings expired.

3/ Preliminary.

Table 10 .- Wheat: Weighted average cash price per bushel, specified markets and dates, 1956-57

Month and date	All classes and grades six markets		No. 2 Dark Hard and Hard Winter Kansas City		No. 1 Dark No. Spring Minneapolis		No. 2 Hard Amber Durum Minneapolis		No. 2 Red Winter St. Louis		No. 1 Soft White Portland 1/	
	1956	1957	1956	1957	1956	1957	1956	1957	1956	1957	1956	1957
	Dol.	Dol.	Dol.	Dol.	Dol.	Dol.	Dol.	Dol.	Dol.	Dol.	Dol.	Dol.
Month												
April	2.44	2.40	2.33	2.30	2.48	2.39	2.67	2.57	2.33	2.21	2.23	2.63
May	2.44	2.34	2.24	2.23	2.48	2.37	2.70	2.50	2.18	2/2.11	2.22	2.58
Week ended												
April 19	2.42	2.39	2.32	2.37	2.45	2.38	2.66	2.55	2/2.35	3/2.22	2.23	2.63
26	2.42	2.37	2.28	2.30	2.48	2.38	2.70	2.53	2/2.29	3/2.26	2.23	2.64
May 3	2.43	2.38	2.26	2.23	2.47	2.40	2.69	2.54	2/2.18	---	2.23	2.64
10	2.44	2.38	2.27	2.23	2.47	2.39	2.70	2.56	2.25	---	2.23	2.61
17	2.45	2.33	2.30	2.25	2.48	2.34	2.69	2.50	---	3/2.11	2.22	2.58
24	2.44	2.34	2.20	2.24	2.50	2.37	2.71	2.47	3/2.16	3/2.11	2.22	2.57
31	2.43	2.32	2.13	2.22	2.48	2.37	2.70	2.42	2.11	---	2.19	2.54
June 7	2.48	2.34	2.19	3/2.20	2.46	2.35	2.71	2.44	---	---	2.18	2.52
14	2.35	2.36	2/2.09	2.24	2.46	2.38	2.60	2.50	---	2.08	2.15	2.50

1/ Average of daily cash quotations.

2/ Only 2 cars.

3/ Only 1 car.

Table 11 .- Wheat: Average closing price per bushel of July futures, specified markets and dates, 1956-57

Period	Chicago		Kansas City		Minneapolis	
	1956	1957	1956	1957	1956	1957
	Dol.	Dol.	Dol.	Dol.	Dol.	Dol.
Month						
April	2.12	2.13	2.10	2.15	2.31	2.27
May	2.06	2.07	2.06	2.08	2.27	2.18
Week ended						
April 19	2.10	2.14	2.08	2.15	2.30	2.27
26	2.13	2.11	2.09	2.13	2.30	2.24
May 3	2.10	2.09	2.09	2.10	2.29	2.21
10	2.06	2.08	2.06	2.08	2.29	2.20
17	2.08	2.09	2.07	2.08	2.29	2.18
24	2.05	2.07	2.05	2.08	2.26	2.17
31	2.03	2.03	2.02	2.06	2.22	2.16
June 7	2.07	2.03	2.05	2.05	2.26	2.15
14	2.08	2.03	2.06	2.05	2.25	2.17

Table 12 - Wheat: Production and farm disposition, United States, 1940-56 1/

Crop year	Production	Total used for seed	Used on farms where grown			Sold
			For seed	Fed to livestock	Home use 2/	
	1,000 bu.	1,000 bu.	1,000 bu.	1,000 bu.	1,000 bu.	1,000 bu.
1940	814,646	74,351	62,047	98,972	10,348	643,279
1941	941,970	62,490	54,004	98,871	9,020	780,075
1942	969,381	65,487	55,040	91,315	7,259	815,767
1943	843,813	77,351	61,571	89,821	5,690	686,731
1944	1,060,111	80,463	63,934	104,011	5,409	886,757
1945	1,107,623	82,006	63,980	98,876	4,470	940,297
1946	1,152,118	86,823	69,039	88,406	3,861	990,812
1947	1,358,911	91,094	72,244	94,766	4,023	1,187,878
1948	1,294,911	95,015	73,046	98,020	3,475	1,120,370
1949	1,098,415	80,851	60,686	84,984	2,903	949,842
1950	1,019,344	87,904	65,478	74,222	2,836	876,808
1951	988,161	88,195	66,194	66,663	2,639	852,665
1952	1,306,440	89,091	68,704	64,860	2,576	1,170,300
1953	1,173,071	69,478	53,216	65,167	2,410	1,052,278
1954	983,900	64,781	47,862	49,639	2,191	884,208
1955	934,731	67,682	47,327	43,575	1,791	842,038
1956 3/	997,207	56,929	41,284	40,038	1,635	914,250

1/ Data for 1909-28 in The Wheat Situation for May 1941, page 16; for 1929-39 in The Wheat Situation, May-June 1949, page 26.
2/ Relates to quantities ground at the mill for use by producers or exchanged for flour.
3/ Preliminary.

Table 13.- Wheat: Prices per bushel in three exporting countries, Friday, mid-month January-June 1957, weekly April-June 1957

Date (Friday)	Hard spring wheat			Soft wheat	
	No. 1 Dark Northern Spring 13 per-cent protein at Duluth 1/ United States	No. 2 Manitoba at Fort William. 2/ 3/ Canada	Hard winter wheat, No. 1 at Galveston 4/ United States	No. 1 Soft White at Portland 1/ United States	Australia 3/ 4/
	Dollars	Dollars	Dollars	Dollars	Dollars
Friday med-month:					
January 18 :	2.38	1.73	2.57	2.53	5/1.53
February 15 :	2.35	1.73	2.54	2.60	5/1.50
March 15 :	2.32	1.73	2.48	2.61	5/---
April 12 :	2.34	1.72	2.44	2.63	5/1.62
May 17 :	2.26	1.67	2.32	2.58	---
June 14 :	2.27	1.66	2.22	2.50	---
Weekly					
April 18 :	2.30	1.72	2.40	2.63	---
26 :	2.31	1.68	2.37	2.64	---
May 3 :	2.32	1.67	2.32	2.64	---
10 :	2.28	1.68	2.28	2.60	---
24 :	2.25	1.68	2.29	2.56	---
31 :	2.25	1.66	2.29	2.54	---
June 7 :	2.28	1.66	2.25	2.51	---
21 :	2.32	1.66	2.25	2.49	---

1/ Spot or to arrive. 2/ Fort William quotation is in store. 3/ Sales to non-contract countries. Converted to United States currency. 4/ F.o.b. ship. 5/ Australian Wheat Board basic selling price for f.a.q. bulk wheat. No price reported for March and none since April.

Table 14.-- Wheat: Supply and disappearance, United States, 1935-56 1/

Year beginning July	Supply				Disappearance					Military pro-curement 4/	Exports 5/	Ship-ments 6/	Total
	Carryover 2/	Production	Imports 3/	Total	Continental United States								
					Processed for food	Seed	Industrial	Feed	Total				
	1,000 bushels	1,000 bushels	1,000 bushels	1,000 bushels	1,000 bushels	1,000 bushels	1,000 bushels	1,000 bushels	1,000 bushels	1,000 bushels	1,000 bushels	1,000 bushels	1,000 bushels
1935	145,889	628,227	34,748	808,864	490,067	87,479	55	83,343	660,944	--	4,440	3,047	668,431
1936	140,433	629,880	34,616	804,929	493,327	95,896	59	100,149	689,431	--	9,584	3,072	702,087
1937	83,167	873,914	746	957,827	489,440	93,060	69	114,856	697,425	--	103,889	3,406	804,720
1938	153,107	919,913	347	1,073,367	496,189	74,225	103	141,690	712,207	--	108,082	3,063	823,352
1939	250,015	741,210	332	991,557	488,758	72,946	89	101,127	662,920	--	45,258	3,658	711,836
1940	279,721	814,646	3,562	1,097,929	489,422	74,351	100	111,772	675,645		33,866	3,685	713,196
1941	384,733	941,970	3,704	1,330,407	472,906	62,490	1,676	114,254	651,326	16,133	27,774	4,399	699,632
1942	630,775	969,381	1,127	1,601,283	494,971	65,487	54,437	305,771	920,666	25,245	30,960	5,515	982,386
1943	618,897	843,813	136,448	1,599,158	477,287	77,351	108,125	511,233	1,173,996	62,762	42,734	3,111	1,282,603
1944	316,555	1,060,111	42,384	1,419,050	472,675	80,463	83,132	300,095	936,365	150,147	49,106	4,292	1,139,870
1945	279,180	1,107,623	2,037	1,388,840	473,733	82,006	21,302	296,548	873,589	90,883	320,025	4,257	1,288,754
1946	100,086	1,152,118	84	1,252,288	479,361	86,823	58	177,525	743,767	92,459	388,045	4,180	1,168,451
1947	83,837	1,358,911	149	1,442,897	484,060	91,094	693	178,309	754,156	148,613	340,221	3,964	1,246,954
1948	195,943	1,294,911	1,530	1,492,384	471,483	95,015	193	107,348	672,039	181,518	327,827	3,715	1,185,099
1949	307,285	1,098,415	2,237	1,407,937	484,182	80,851	192	111,258	676,483	123,526	179,213	4,001	983,223
1950	424,714	1,019,344	11,919	1,455,977	479,550	87,904	192	108,808	676,454	41,267	334,513	3,872	1,056,106
1951	399,871	988,161	31,609	1,419,641	481,084	88,195	930	102,401	672,610	16,714	470,347	3,992	1,163,663
1952	255,978	1,306,440	21,602	1,584,020	473,613	89,091	175	82,480	645,359	13,620	315,652	3,845	978,476
1953	605,544	1,173,071	5,537	1,784,152	472,662	69,478	178	76,637	618,955	12,034	215,704	3,953	850,646
1954	933,506	983,900	4,197	1,921,603	473,070	64,781	230	60,053	598,134	9,882	273,419	3,990	835,425
1955 7/	1,036,178	934,731	9,933 (8,000)	1,980,842 (2,038,000)	468,728	67,682	678	52,148	589,236	8,213	8/346,093	3,918	947,460
1956 7/	1,033,382	997,207				56,929							

1/ Includes flour and other wheat products in terms of wheat. 2/ Prior to 1937 some new wheat included; beginning with 1937 only old-crop wheat is shown in all stocks positions. The figure for July 1, 1937, including the new wheat, is 102.8 million bushels, which is used as year-end carryover in the 1936-37 marketing year. 3/ Imports include full-duty wheat, wheat imported for feed, and dutiable flour and other wheat products in terms of wheat. They exclude wheat imported for milling in bond and export as flour, also flour free for export. 4/ Includes procurement for both civilian relief feeding and for military foor use; military takings for civilian feeding in occupied areas measured at times of procurement, not at time of shipment overseas. 5/ Exports as here used in addition to commercial exports of wheat, flour, and other wheat products, include U.S.DA. flour procurement rather than deliveries for export. Beginning with 1941-42, actual exports, including those for civilian feeding in occupied areas (deliveries for export) of wheat, flour and other wheat products, in million bushels, were as follows: 27.9; 27.8; 42.6; 144.4; 390.6; 397.4; 485.9; 504.0; 299.1; 366.1; 475.3; 317.8; 217.0; 274.3 and 346.1. 6/ To Alaska, Hawaii, Puerto Rico, Guam, Samoa, Virgin Islands and Wake Island; partly estimated. 7/ Preliminary. 8/ Includes exports of 2,788,000 bushels for relief or charity by individuals and private agencies. 9/ For the period July-December 1955, known disappearance from the July 1 supply, without an allowance for quantities fed, is about 12 million bushels larger than that indicated by January 1 stocks. This discrepancy may be accounted for by possible inexactness in data, including some duplication in stocks reported in the various positions by different agencies. 10/ Includes exports of 2,220,000 bushels for relief or charity.

Table 15.- Wheat: Supply and disappearance, United States, July-December and January-June periods, 1944-56 1/

Period	Carryover stocks 2/	Production	Imports 3/	Total supply	Processed for food	Total used for seed	Industrial	Feed	Total domestic	Military procurement 4/	Exports	Shipments 6/	Total disappearance
	1,000 bushels	1,000 bushels	1,000 bushels	1,000 bushels	1,000 bushels	1,000 bushels	1,000 bushels	1,000 bushels	1,000 bushels	1,000 bushels	1,000 bushels	1,000 bushels	1,000 bushels
1944 July-Dec.	316,555	1,060,111	37,634	1,414,300	233,467	58,475	54,390	173,234	519,566	41,879	22,918	1,590	585,953
Jan.-June	828,347	—	4,750	833,097	239,203	21,988	28,742	126,861	416,799	108,268	26,188	2,662	553,917
1945 July-Dec.	279,180	1,107,663	1,925	1,388,728	256,010	59,109	19,530	160,340	494,989	61,832	147,973	2,014	706,808
Jan.-June	681,920	—	112	682,032	217,723	22,897	1,772	136,208	378,600	29,051	172,052	2,243	581,946
1946 July-Dec.	100,086	1,152,118	38	1,252,242	276,695	63,192	11	101,816	441,714	37,949	127,873	2,220	609,756
Jan.-June	642,486	—	46	642,532	202,666	23,631	47	75,709	302,053	54,510	200,172	1,960	558,695
1947 July-Dec.	83,837	1,358,911	53	1,442,801	263,476	67,210	603	54,947	366,236	67,020	186,711	2,067	642,034
Jan.-June	800,767	—	96	800,863	220,584	23,684	90	123,362	367,920	81,593	153,510	1,897	604,920
1948 July-Dec.	195,943	1,294,911	48	1,490,902	248,436	67,703	92	34,150	350,381	107,588	166,557	1,831	626,357
Jan.-June	864,545	—	1,482	866,027	223,047	27,312	101	71,198	321,658	73,930	161,270	1,884	559,742
1949 July-Dec.	307,285	1,098,415	182	1,405,882	250,517	57,123	100	24,105	331,845	102,543	69,248	1,938	505,574
Jan.-June	900,308	—	2,055	902,363	233,665	23,728	92	87,153	344,638	20,983	109,965	2,063	477,649
1950 July-Dec.	424,714	1,019,344	2,243	1,446,301	247,206	60,724	98	18,085	326,113	16,566	99,299	1,827	443,805
Jan.-June	1,002,496	—	9,676	1,012,172	238,344	27,180	94	90,723	350,341	24,701	235,214	2,045	612,301
1951 July-Dec.	399,871	988,161	17,434	1,405,466	286,254	61,793	727	16,824	325,598	9,371	214,608	1,998	551,575
Jan.-June	853,891	—	14,175	868,066	234,830	26,402	203	85,577	347,012	7,343	255,739	1,994	612,088
1952 July-Dec.	255,978	1,306,440	17,669	1,580,087	245,371	61,891	73	743	308,078	6,307	154,436	1,818	470,639
Jan.-June	1,109,448	—	3,933	1,113,381	288,242	27,200	102	81,737	337,281	7,313	161,216	2,027	507,837
1953 July-Dec.	605,514	1,173,071	1,581	1,780,196	243,728	49,329	101	36,567	329,725	6,154	108,047	2,029	445,955
Jan.-June	1,334,241	—	3,956	1,338,197	228,934	20,149	77	40,070	289,230	5,880	107,657	1,924	404,691
1954 July-Dec.	933,506	983,900	885	1,918,291	244,276	47,761	64	15,482	307,603	5,258	122,286	1,939	437,086
Jan.-June	1,481,205	—	3,312	1,484,517	228,794	17,000	166	44,571	290,531	4,624	151,133	2,051	448,339
1955 7/ July-Dec.	1,036,178	934,731	3,174	1,974,083	242,460	48,215	202	2/ -11,560	279,317	3,926	8/ 121,987	1,903	407,133
Jan.-June	1,566,950	—	6,759	1,573,709	226,268	19,467	476	63,708	309,919	4,287	224,106	2,015	540,327
1956 7/ July-Dec.	1,033,382	997,207	3,034	2,033,623	241,200	41,534	291	9,155	293,180	4,657	10/247,560	1,960	546,357
Jan.-June	1,487,266	—				15,395							

See table 14 for footnotes.

Table 16.- Wheat: Stocks in the United States on April 1, 1951-57

	1,000 bu.	1,000 bu.	1,000 bu.	1,000 bu.	1,000 bu.	1,000 bu.	1,000 bu.
Farm 1/	217,127	199,174	270,928	297,139	211,358	216,741	165,959
Interior mills, elevators and warehouses 2/	200,642	112,337	247,706	380,137	461,579	503,572	449,709
Terminals (commercial) 3/	193,663	124,865	217,258	298,934	351,913	366,412	360,702
Merchant mills and mill elevators 4/	101,052	80,760	101,691	104,778	101,475	102,455	108,918
Commodity Credit Corporation 5/	3,156	2,037	4,351	47,483	122,509	132,022	102,380
Total							

1/ Estimates of Crop Reporting Board.

2/ All off-farm storage not otherwise designated.

3/ Commercial stocks reported by Grain Division, AMS at 43 terminal cities.

4/ Mills reporting to the Bureau of the Census on millings and stocks of flour.

5/ Owned by CCC and stored in bins or other storage owned or controlled by CCC; also CCC-owned wheat in transit and in Canadian elevators. Other wheat owned by CCC as well as wheat outstand under loan is included in other stocks positions.

Table 17.- Wheat: CCC sales or other disposition, July 1, 1956-May 1957

Item	Disposition	
	1,000 bushels	1,000 bushels
Domestic		
Sales	23,730	
Donations	5,532	29,262
Exports		
Sales 1/	125,856	
Donations	11,065	
Transfers through International Cooperative Administration	4,301	
International barter	61,972	203,194
Fire, theft, spoilage, etc.		670
Total		233,126

1/ Include noncommercial sales to foreign governments as well as commercial sales. Exclude sales of wheat registered with CCC under the payment-in-kind program, which from the beginning of the program September 4, 1956 through May 29, 1957, totaled 328,781,091 bushels. However, sales do include wheat sold in redemption of certificates under the payment-in-kind program which during May totaled 22,850,862 bushels and from the beginning of the program through May totaled 84,667,26 bushels.

Commodity Stabilization Service

Table 18.- Storage capacity of elevators reporting commercial grain stocks,
by regions and cities, June 1, 1956-57 (All grains)

Region	:	Cities	: June 1, 1956	: June 1, 1957
	:		: 1,000 bushels	: 1,000 bushels
ATLANTIC COAST	:	Baltimore, Md......................:	13,781	: 13,781
	:	Boston, Mass.......................:	1,880	: 1,880
	:	New York, N. Y.....................:	4,450	: 4,450
	:	Norfolk, Va........................:	2,000	: 4,250
	:	Philadelphia, Pa...................:	5,135	: 5,335
	:	Portland, Maine....................:	1,500	: 1,500
	:	Total...........................:	28,746	: 31,196
GULF COAST	:	Galveston, Texas...................:	6,864	: 6,864
	:	Houston, Texas.....................:	3,200	: 3,200
	:	New Orleans, La....................:	5,122	: 5,122
	:	Mobile, Ala........................:	1,450	: 1,450
	:	Corpus Christi, Texas..............:	2,000	: 2,000
	:	Total...........................:	18,636	: 18,636
NORTHWESTERN AND	:	Duluth, Minn. - Superior, Wis......:	60,500	: 60,500
UPPER LAKE	:	Minneapolis, Minn..................:	89,829	: 90,333
	:	Total...........................:	150,329	: 150,833
LOWER LAKE	:	Buffalo, N. Y......................:	35,250	: 35,340
	:	Chicago, Ill.......................:	54,200	: 68,060
	:	Milwaukee, Wis.....................:	7,605	: 7,605
	:	Toledo, Ohio.......................:	16,289	: 16,289
	:	Total...........................:	113,344	: 127,294
EAST CENTRAL	:	Cincinnati, Ohio...................:	2,550	: 2,550
	:	Indianapolis, Ind.................:	13,300	: 13,300
	:	Louisville, Ky....................:	5,380	: 5,380
	:	Memphis, Tenn......................:	2,700	: 2,700
	:	Nashville, Tenn....................:	1,959	: 1,959
	:	Peoria, Ill........................:	4,500	: 4,886
	:	St. Louis, Mo......................:	22,125	: 22,125
	:	Total...........................:	52,514	: 52,900
WEST CENTRAL,	:	Amarillo, Texas....................:	10,245	: 12,095
SOUTHWESTERN, AND	:	Burlington, Iowa...................:	1,200	: 1,200
WESTERN	:	Dallas, Texas......................:	2,300	: 2,300
	:	Denver, Colo.......................:	2,071	: 2,071
	:	Des Moines, Iowa...................:	8,330	: 8,330
	:	Enid, Okla.........................:	61,375	: 61,375
	:	Fort Worth, Texas..................:	27,175	: 35,175
	:	Hutchinson, Kans...................:	32,690	: 32,750
	:	Kansas City, Mo....................:	61,730	: 61,730
	:	Lincoln, Nebr......................:	20,805	: 25,075
	:	Lubbock, Texas.....................:	17,360	: 23,250
	:	Ogden, Utah........................:	3,000	: 3,000
	:	Omaha, Nebr. - Council Bluffs, Iowa:	28,235	: 29,790
	:	St. Joseph, Mo.....................:	4,500	: 4,500
	:	Salina, Kans.......................:	22,750	: 23,750
	:	Sioux City, Iowa...................:	6,175	: 6,325
	:	Wichita, Kans......................:	43,000	: 43,000
	:	Total...........................:	352,941	: 375,716
PACIFIC COAST	:	Portland and Columbia River........:	68,335	: 64,500
	:	Spokane, Wash......................:	2,102	: 2,102
	:	Seattle and Tacoma, Wash...........:	14,511	: 14,511
	:	San Francisco and Bay Region, Calif.:	11,336	: 11,959
	:	Total...........................:	96,284	: 93,072
	:			
	:	Grand total.......................:	812,794	: 849,647

Table 19.- Wheat: Inspected receipts, by classes and grades, United States, 1955-56 1/

Class and subclass	No. 1 Heavy	No. 1	No. 2	No. 3	No. 4	No. 5	Sample	Total	Percentage grading No. 2 or better
				--1,000 bushels--					Percent
Dark northern spring..	41,233	87,166	34,173	21,432	17,925	4,764	2,449	209,142	78
Northern spring.......	1,260	3,632	3,028	2,150	2,353	1,498	1,887	15,808	50
Red spring............	35	6	7	0	0	4	4	56	86
Hard amber durum......	0	3,225	2,908	1,038	344	117	75	7,707	80
Amber durum...........	0	681	2,529	1,478	559	170	183	5,600	57
Durum.................	0	92	365	324	185	80	105	1,151	40
Red durum.............	0	2	2	0	0	0	0	4	100
Dark hard winter......	0	263,144	39,009	7,541	1,746	555	2,374	314,369	96
Hard winter..........	0	249,038	63,512	8,919	2,531	2,031	8,327	334,358	93
Yellow hard winter....	0	3,589	3,768	185	33	22	76	7,673	96
Red winter...........	0	43,897	70,616	16,258	2,712	908	2,067	136,458	84
Western red..........	0	426	738	55	9	2	6	1,236	94
Hard white...........	0	6,129	783	126	94	9	54	7,195	96
Soft white...........	0	30,669	26,914	8,334	411	111	450	66,889	86
White club...........	0	18,705	25,031	2,185	137	72	107	46,237	95
Western white........	0	12,178	7,169	590	74	35	126	20,172	96
Mixed wheat..........	0	15,823	7,803	1,591	603	392	870	27,082	87
Amber mixed durum....	0	372	163	92	46	11	17	701	76
Mixed durum..........	0	22	52	70	33	8	9	194	38
Total.............	42,528	738,796	288,570	72,368	29,795	10,789	19,186	1,202,032	89

1/ Carlot receipts have been converted to bushels on the basis that 1 carlot equals 1,850 bushels.

Based on reports of carlot inspections by licensed inspectors at all markets. Does not include cargo or truck receipts.

INDEX OF TABLES

U. S. Department of Agriculture
Washington 25, D. C .

Penalty for private use to avoid payment of postage $300

NOTICE
If you no longer need this publication,
check here ╱▔▔╱ return this sheet,
and your name will be dropped from
the mailing list.

If your address should be changed,
write the new address on this sheet
and return the whole sheet to:

Administrative Services Division (ML)
Agricultural Marketing Service
U. S. Department of Agriculture
Washington 25, D. C.

Grain and Feed Statistics Through 1956, Statistical Bul-
letin No. 159, Revised May 1957 is now available. Single copies
may be obtained from Office of Information, U. S. Department of
Agriculture, Washington 25, D. C. Additional copies may be purchased from the Superintendent of Documents, Government Printing
Office, Washington 25, D. C., at 50 cents per copy.

The Wheat Situation is published in
February, April, June, August and October.
The next issue will be released August 22,
1957.